FIRST 15 LESSONS

BASS GUITAR

by Jon Liebman

Includes Audio & Video Access

This purpose of this book is to provide the beginning bassist with a hands-on approach to the fundamentals of good bass playing. As in all of my books, as well as my online bass lessons, I have presented you with a sequence of practical exercises to provide not only technical instruction, but examples that are musically satisfying and enjoyable to play. I've also included several examples from well-known songs to further enhance your real-world learning experience. Note that the lessons progress sequentially, with each lesson building on the previous material, so be sure to go through them in order.

Congratulations on your decision to become a bass player! Welcome to the low end!

—Jon Liebman

ISBN 978-1-5400-0293-8

PLAYBACK+
Speed · Pitch · Balance · Loop

To access audio, video, and extra content visit:
www.halleonard.com/mylibrary

Enter Code
6214-0738-2265-0869

HAL•LEONARD®
7777 W. BLUEMOUND RD. P.O. BOX 13819 MILWAUKEE, WI 53213

Visit Hal Leonard Online at
www.halleonard.com

FIRST, A FEW THINGS YOU NEED TO KNOW

Before we begin, let's take care of a few "housekeeping" items. First, let's make sure you're holding your bass correctly and using proper posture. If you're wearing a strap, make sure your bass hangs over your body at the same height when you're both standing and sitting. I recommend wearing the bass rather high, as that position makes for more efficient placement of the hands, particularly the left hand (for the sake of simplicity, I refer to the right and left hands as if you are right-handed; if you're left-handed, adjust accordingly). Someday, when you're a big rock star and decide to sling the instrument way down over your knees, go for it! In the meantime, let's begin by holding it at a level that will work most efficiently with the position of your hands.

Next, be sure your bass is in tune. A conventional bass has four strings. From lowest to highest, those strings are E, A, D, and G. (Note that when I say "lowest to highest," I'm referring to pitch, not physical location. The E string, for example, is lowest in pitch, but furthest from the floor.) While there are several ways to tune your bass, the easiest and most common way is to use a tuner. It's pretty easy to get a hold of a decent, inexpensive tuner and tune up to E–A–D–G.

A free online tuner comes with this book! Simply visit **www.halleonard.com/mylibrary** and enter the code found on page 1 to access it.

As for the actual plucking of the strings, some bassists use their right-hand fingers, while others play exclusively with a pick. It really comes down to style and preference, as well as what the music calls for. Most jazz and R&B players tend to use their fingers—typically, the index and middle fingers—while a lot of rock and heavy-metal players use a pick. Throughout this book, you'll probably have an easier time using your fingers, but if you'd like to experiment with a pick, by all means, give it a try.

Keeping in mind that you are a beginning bass player, maybe even a beginning musician, I've kept the music notation fairly straightforward. Let's go over a few basic topics in regard to reading music.

For starters, music is divided into equal units called *measures*, or *bars*. All of the exercises in this book are written in what's known as *4/4 time*. The "4" at the top of this *time signature* tells us that there are four beats in every measure. The bottom number—in this case, also a 4—tells us that each beat is the length of a *quarter note*. The quarter note is so named because each one is equal to exactly one quarter of the time span of the measure. It's actually a pretty simple concept, very much like the basic fractions you learned in grade school.

Take a look at the following example. Notice the first measure has only one note, called a *whole note*. Whenever you see a note like this (i.e., an open circle all by itself), you know it's a whole note and lasts for four beats, or a whole measure. Measure 2 has two notes, each with a duration of two beats. These notes, the open circles with stems attached, are called *half notes* (starting to see a pattern yet?). Now look at measure 3. Each note, a filled-in circle with a stem, is called a *quarter note*. We know that when we divide anything into four equal parts, each part makes up one quarter of the whole. Well, it's the same thing in music: four quarter notes equal one measure.

Now let's take it one step further: a note that's half the length of a quarter note is—you guessed it!—an *eighth note*. In measure 4, there are eight eighth notes grouped in fours, each group connected by a *beam*. Instead of counting "1, 2, 3, 4," we sub-divide each beat, counting "1-and, 2-and, 3-and, 4-and." When you see a lone eighth note, one that is not beamed to another note, it's indicated by a *flag*, as in the fifth measure. The combination of eighth notes and quarter notes still adds up to four beats.

Ex. 1

Like anything else, learning a new skill takes some time. The online video that accompanies this book will be a big help.

Sometimes in music, we want to leave some space between the notes. When we're not playing, we're "resting." In the example below, the first two bars show you what quarter rests look like, and the second two bars show you what eighth rests look like. All the while, we're still counting "1-and, 2-and, 3-and, 4-and." The length of each measure does not change.

Ex. 2

Let's discuss one more thing before we move on: *tablature*. Take a look at the example below. Notice the four lines with the word "tab" (short for "tablature") to the left. These four lines correspond to the four strings on the bass, lowest to highest: E, A, D, and G. The numbers tell you what fret to play on each string. Tablature is a helpful way for you to play the notes if you're not yet adept at reading music.

Ex. 3

In this book, we will be using a combination of standard notation and tablature called "rhythm tab," an easy-to-understand format that will get you playing and reading bass music quickly. However, you are also encouraged to learn how to read standard music notation. In rhythm tab, rhythmic stems and circles are attached to tab numbers on one staff. Here is the previous figure now shown in rhythm tab notation:

Ex. 4

Now that you've got an overview of some of the basics, let's play some music! If you're ready to start grooving, turn the page and let's do it!

LESSON 2

GETTING STARTED: GROOVIN' ON OPEN STRINGS

Let's dive right in and play some music! In this lesson, you'll see how much you can actually groove while using only the open strings on your bass. We're going to play several variations of a *12-bar blues*, one of the primary building blocks of much of today's music.

As you play the example below, concentrate on letting only the desired string ring out, using your fingers on both hands to mute the other strings. The more experienced you become as a bass player, the better you'll get at mastering this technique.

As for your right hand, start plucking by alternating your first two fingers, beginning with the second finger, holding your fingers in a straight, downward position. Eventually, you'll find yourself experimenting with different right-hand plucking techniques. As your playing progresses, you'll figure out what works best for you, depending on the situation. For this example, though, play 2–1, 2–1, etc.

Let's get started. Here's a nice, easy blues. Note that the *chord symbols* above the staff (A7, D7, etc.) are provided for reference or for someone to accompany you on guitar, piano, or another chordal instrument.

Before we begin, I want to call your attention to the heavy bar lines, with two dots, at the beginning and near the end of the following example. These are called *repeat* signs. Good sightreaders make note of repeat signs, remembering their locations, and returning back to them upon seeing the matching symbol at the end of the section. In this case, the notation tells you to play the first 12 bars, then to repeat them, after which you'll continue to the following bar, without stopping. You'll find repeat signs on nearly all the examples in this book, as you're encouraged to practice them repeatedly until you can play them proficiently. On the accompanying audio tracks, however, the examples are played without repeats.

Ex. 1

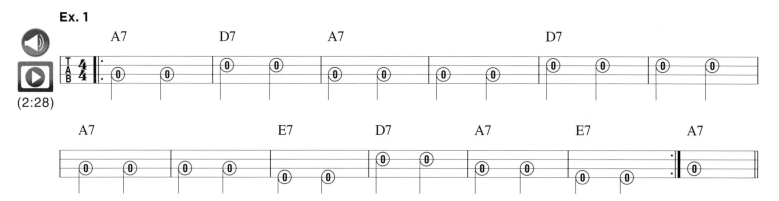

(2:28)

You just played a 12-bar blues! Keep practicing this example with the goal of playing it smoothly and with a steady beat.

When you're ready, let's take it up a notch by going through the following variations. In each example, I've given you the first four bars of the 12-bar blues as a head start, but with each variation, I want you to play through the entire form, as we did in the previous example. Notice the dots next to some of the notes. When you see a *dotted note*, it's telling you to hold the note for its entire duration, plus another one half of its original value. A dotted quarter note, for example, means you hold the note for one-and-a-half beats. Don't worry—you'll feel it!

Ex. 2

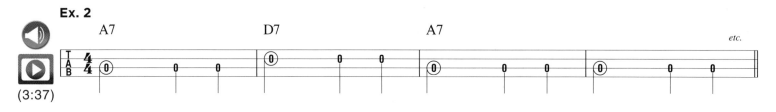

(3:37)

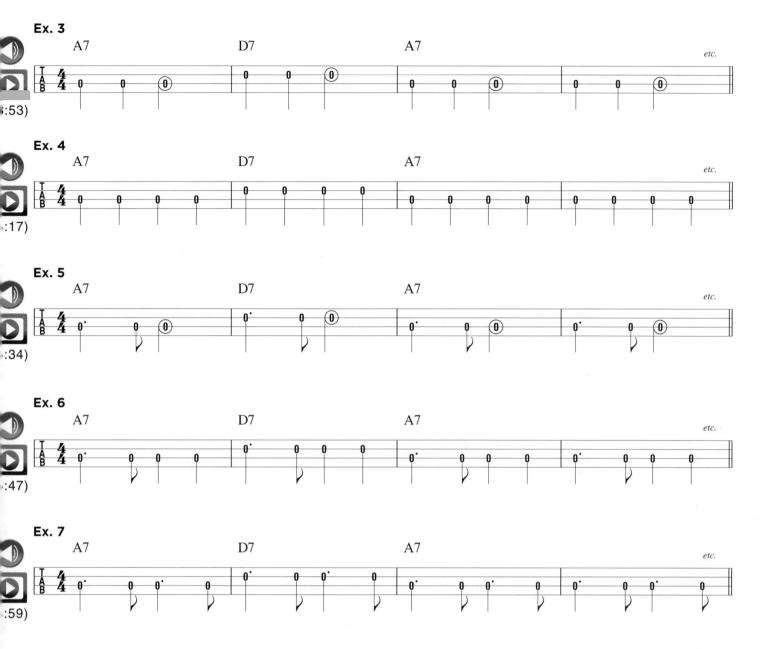

Now let's repeat the whole process, this time beginning on the D string. Everything is played exactly like the previous examples, except one string higher. That way, you'll start to get some familiarity with all four strings. You'll find the online audio and video to this book to be very helpful.

Remember to concentrate on sounding only one note at a time. Sometimes, you'll find yourself muting the strings with your left hand, and other times with the right, depending on where it's needed. Also, remember to alternate your right-hand fingers: 2–1, 2–1, etc.

When you practice the bass, you should use a metronome to help develop a good sense of time. A *metronome* provides a steady, constant click at any tempo. Practice new material at slow tempos first, then gradually increase the speed. Strive to lock in with the click just as you would with the drummer in a band. Solid timing: it's your most important job as a bass player!

A free online metronome comes with this book! Simply visit **www.halleonard.com/mylibrary** and enter the code found on page 1 to access it.

Continue working on these examples until it starts to feel like you're actually playing the blues. Be sure to put in whatever amount of time is necessary. I've included quite a bit of variety to keep things interesting. When you're ready to move on, we'll start giving the left hand some stuff to do, too!

THE 1–5 PATTERN: A BASS-PLAYING ESSENTIAL

As a bass player, the most important note you'll ever play is the root of the chord. The rest of the band looks to us to provide the bottom, the foundation upon which everything else is built.

The second most important—and arguably the second most frequent—note you'll play is the 5th. By *5th*, I mean the fifth note of the chord's scale. In a C chord, for example, the root (1) is C, and the 5th (5) is G. It's really just that simple. Once you hear it, you'll instantly recognize it. Bass players everywhere know all about playing "1–5, 1–5" all day long.

Playing the root-5th (1–5) pattern on the bass is pretty easy. Start by playing the root of the chord, and then play the note that's one string higher and two frets up. Take a look at the tab staff and you'll see what I mean. Let's play the following example, slow and steady.

Ex. 1

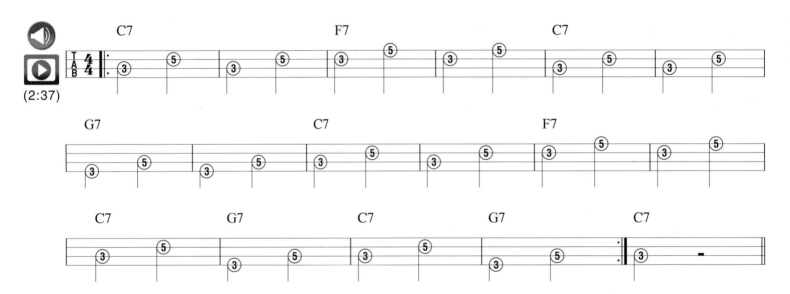

(2:37)

Now let's play it again, but with a few variations to the rhythm. The more ways you practice a piece of music, the better you'll get those notes solidly under your fingers. It's more fun, too! If you're not a strong sight-reader, don't let the notation intimidate you. The rhythms are pretty simple. Play along with the audio track, and you'll get it in no time.

Remember: the goal of this book is to start you out with the fundamentals of bass playing in a way that will have you grooving right from the beginning. Practice this lesson until it sounds like you're making music, rather than reading notes. Don't forget to use the online audio and video that accompany this book, as they will help you a lot. When you're ready, let's move on to the "other" kind of 1–5 pattern.

SAME-FRET 1–5 PATTERNS: THERE *IS* A DIFFERENCE

In Lesson 3, we talked about the 1–5 pattern being one of the most important building blocks of playing the bass. Here, we'll look at another way to play that pattern. Quite often, you'll want to play the 5th **below** the root note, rather than above it. (For you theory buffs, it's technically a 4th lower than the root, but don't worry about that now. It's still the 5th of the chord and thus it satisfies our 1–5 requirement.)

In this case, the two notes are on the same fret, which makes the pattern more challenging to play. You need to get comfortable shifting your finger across the fret in just the right way so that only the intended note is articulated. It'll take some practice, but it's absolutely required. The online video will help, too. Let's play the following example, combining both kinds of 1–5 patterns.

Ex. 1

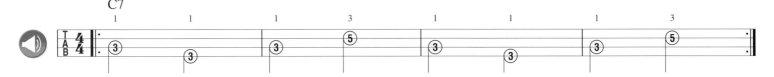

Now let's play it again, this time starting on the D string.

Ex. 2

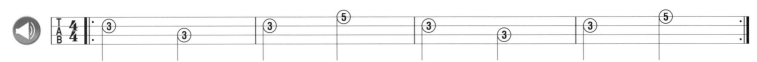

In the example below, you'll play an entire blues form, using nothing but 1–5 patterns (except for a couple of octaves that I threw in toward the end). Remember to concentrate on letting only the desired note ring out, without any extraneous tones or string noise. It takes concentration and diligence, but every great bass player was once where you are right now, so keep at it till you get it!

Ex. 3

(2:22)

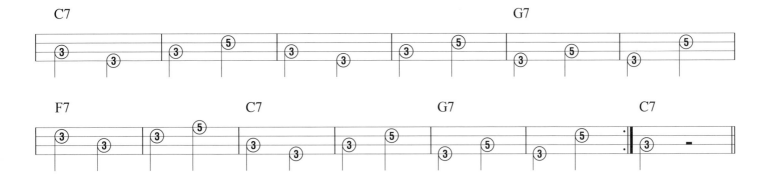

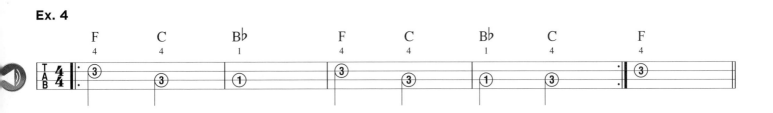

Now I'm going to introduce another variation of our same-fret 1–5 pattern. In this case, instead of starting with our first finger, we'll start with our fourth finger. As before, you'll need to master the movement of your hand so that you're only playing the note you want. The difference this time is that you'll be using your pinky instead of your index finger.

Ex. 4

Feels different, doesn't it? In the next example, let's combine the first- and fourth-finger patterns.

Ex. 5

(5:26)

Ex. 6

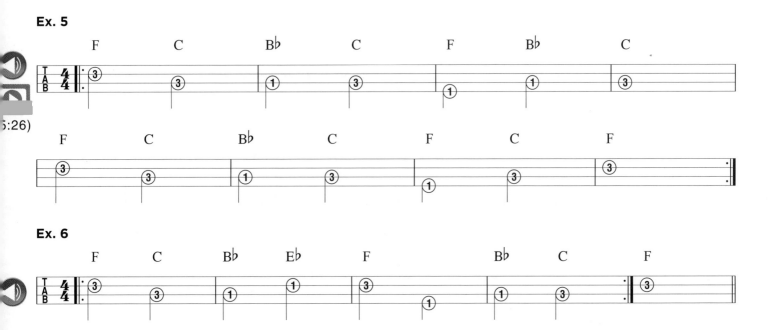

Don't get frustrated if you can't make these maneuvers right away. These fingerings take lots of practice, so keep pluggin' away. Before you know it, they'll feel natural and you'll be thinking "1–5, 1–5" in your sleep. That's when you'll know you're a true bass player!

LESSON 5

SINGLE-STRING GROOVES

In this lesson, we're going to play some "feel good" grooves, each one on a single string. Let's start with a simple three-note pattern just to get the notes under your fingers.

Ex. 1

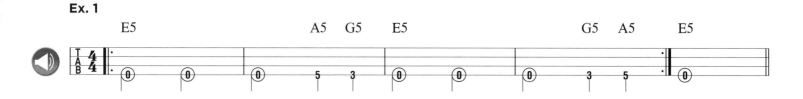

Now we'll vary the rhythm a little bit. It's amazing how such a small modification can really make the music groove.

Ex. 2

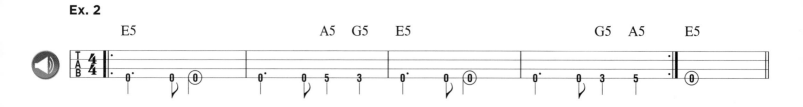

Here's a slight variation to the previous examples, with the line just a little busier:

Ex. 3

(0:53)

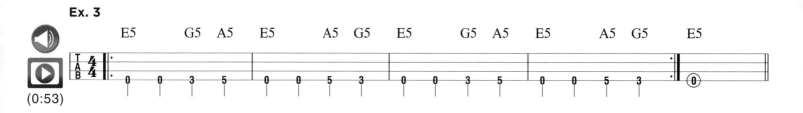

And now with the variation in rhythm:

Ex. 4

(1:18)

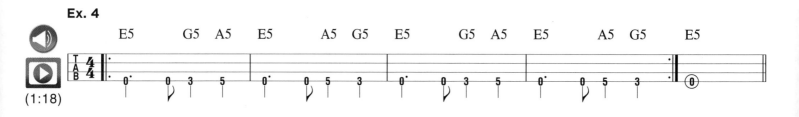

Whaddaya know... you're grooving! Let's mix it up a little more, starting from the top and moving down.

Ex. 5

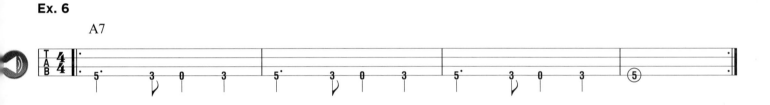

And now, a little more rhythmically interesting:

Ex. 6

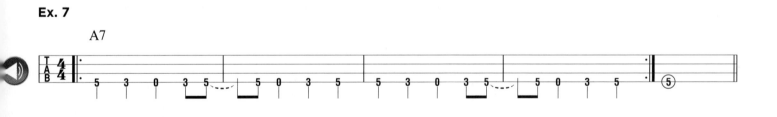

In this next example, notice that the notes between bars 1–2 and bars 3–4 are connected. This notation, known as a *tie*, means that you hold the note for its entire duration plus the duration of the note to which it's tied. In other words, you only pluck the string once, but you hold the note for the duration of both notes. Again, you'll hear it and you'll feel it.

Ex. 7

These exercises show how you can take the simplest pattern and make it groove. Consider also that each example is made up of just three notes!

Further, notice that the only string we've used is the E string. Keep working on these examples until you've got them down. Before moving on, though, I want you to repeat everything we've covered in this lesson on the A, D, and G strings. It'll make your grooving ability four times better!

LESSON 6

PLAYING ACROSS THE FINGERBOARD

This lesson will give you some good practice playing patterns over two or more strings, each within a single position on the bass. In other words, you'll be covering a wider range of notes than before, but you won't need to move up or down the fingerboard.

Let's start with a simple pattern that moves across all four strings, utilizing only the third and fifth frets.

Ex. 1

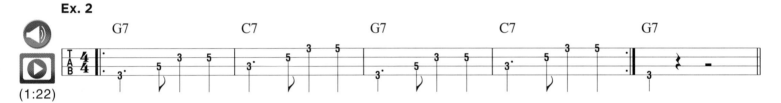

(0:49)

Now that you've got those notes under your fingers, let's vary the rhythm a bit, making it more interesting, musically.

Ex. 2

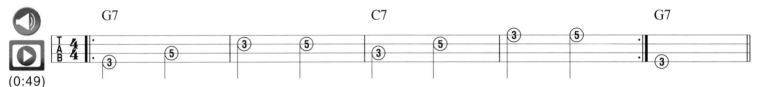

(1:22)

For the next example, you'll need to move up a little higher on the fingerboard, to the fifth and seventh frets. This example will help you get your fingers familiar with the notes. Watch out for the same-fret 1–5 passage at the end of bar 3.

Ex. 3

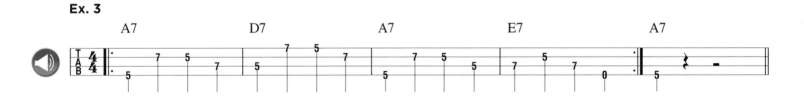

Now let's make it more musical:

Ex. 4

Another thing good bass players often do is outline chords, playing what's known as arpeggios. An *arpeggio* is made up of the individual notes of a chord, played one at a time instead of all at once. The following example demonstrates how to play A7 and D7 arpeggios.

Ex. 5

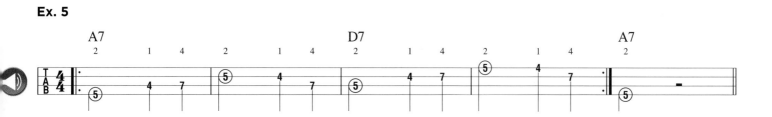

Let's give that exercise a little more movement. As a bass player, you'll find yourself playing this next pattern a lot. You might want to try it in different areas of the fingerboard, too.

Ex. 6

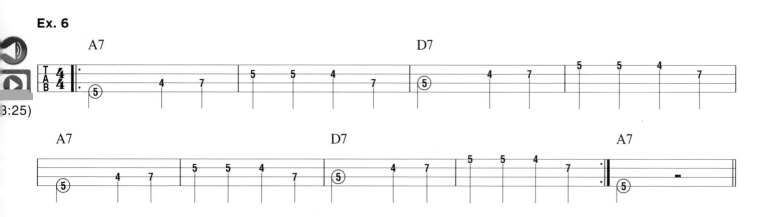

The examples in this lesson will help you play your string crossings cleanly and efficiently. Remember to concentrate on making sure that the only note you hear is the one you want to hear, as well as playing steadily and with a good time feel. It takes a lot of practice, so make sure you listen to the audio tracks and watch the videos to learn how these grooves are supposed to be played. Once you're feeling somewhat proficient playing across the fingerboard, we'll begin working on some basic position shifts.

POSITION SHIFTS

Now let's start getting your hands used to moving up and down the neck of the bass, slowly and gradually.

Here's a simple pattern that starts on frets 3 and 5 and then moves down to frets 1 and 3:

Ex. 1

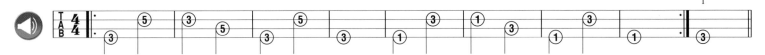

Below are a few variations. These examples are good for both hands.

Ex. 2

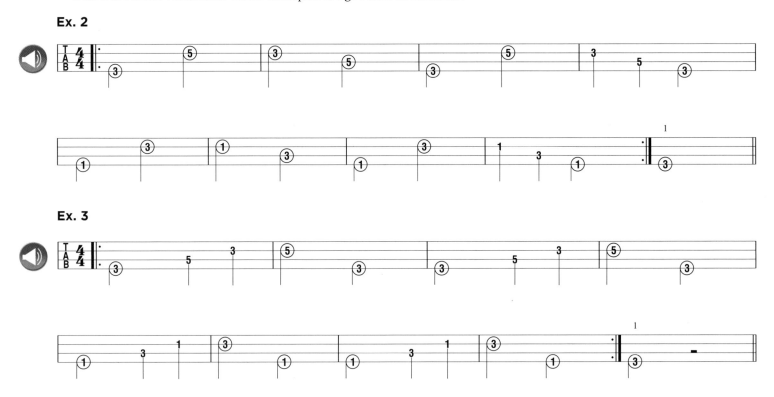

Ex. 3

Ex. 4

In the next example, we'll begin on the third fret as before. This time, though, we'll move **up** the fingerboard, first to the fifth and seventh frets, then to the sixth and eighth frets, and back down. This will be great practice for you!

Ex. 5

(2:17)

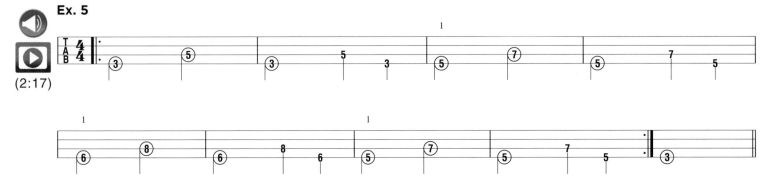

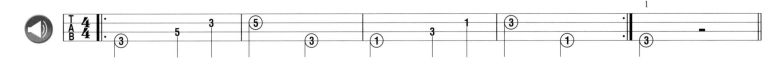

Below is a very common progression. It starts at the fifth and seventh frets and then moves downward. First, let's get comfortable with the notes.

Ex. 6

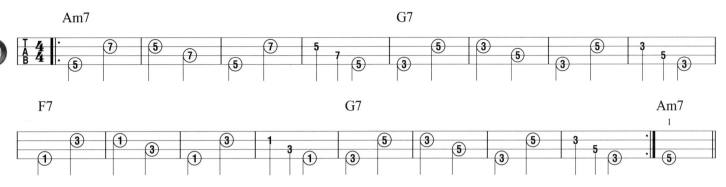

Now let's get a little more active with the rhythm.

Ex. 7

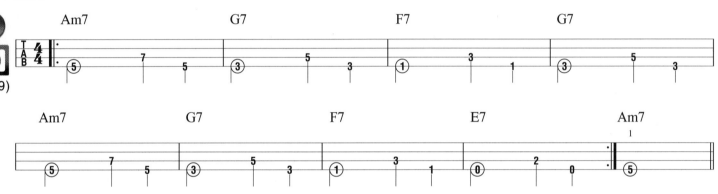

Playing with dotted rhythms gives it a very different feel.

Ex. 8

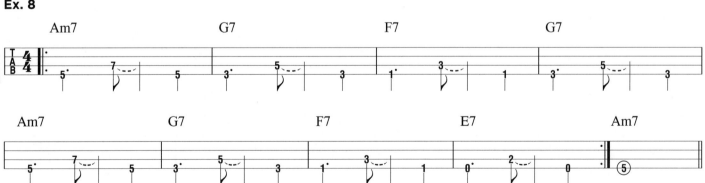

Continue working on this lesson until shifting positions starts to feel natural. It'll take some work, so be sure to put in the time. Those shifts need to be smooth and effortless. When you're ready to move on, we'll combine the techniques we've covered so far and play an entire song.

Demo   Play-Along

"SMOOTH"

It's time to learn your first full song—"Smooth" by Santana. Pay extra close attention to the "road map" here. There are several instances of repeated sections, so be sure to make note of the repeat signs—beginnings and endings. Otherwise, you won't be with the rest of the band. This piece also makes use of first and second *endings*, which may be new to you. Notice on page 17, at the Interlude, the bracketed line above the staff with the number "1" tells you to play those four bars the first time around. Once you get to the repeat sign, go back to the Verse on the first page (did you make note of the repeat sign when you started playing that section?) and play it through again. This time, however, after playing the Chorus, you'll jump to the second ending at the end of the third bar, indicated by the bracketed line over the bar with the number "2." But don't relax yet! The next section, where it says "Guitar Solo," also has a repeat sign in front of it, with another set of endings.

Intro

Verse

Chorus

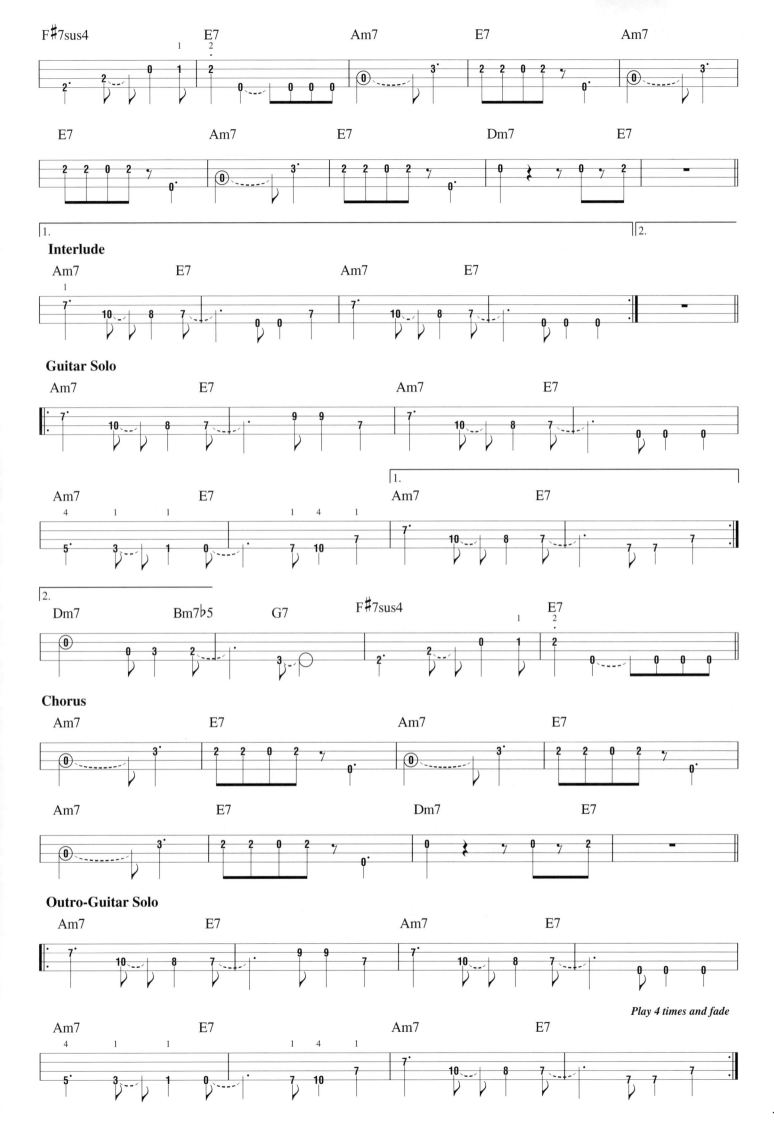

CHROMATICS

So far, we've worked on various patterns and grooves, typically playing on the third and fifth frets, the first and third frets, the fifth and seventh frets, and so on. Do you know what lies in between those frets? That's right... more frets! In this lesson, we'll focus on playing inside those gaps as we move up and down the fingerboard, one fret at a time.

The interval from one fret to its closest neighbor, up or down, is called a *half step*. A succession of half steps from A to A or from C to C, for example, is called the *chromatic scale*. The following exercises will give you lots of practice playing chromatic lines, each within the context of a groove.

Our first example illustrates chromatic playing in conjunction with open strings. This type of bass line works very well in jazz, blues, and other styles.

Ex. 1

(2:16)

Before moving on, play this same line but beginning on the D string, then on the G string. Everything is the same—frets, open strings, etc.—you just move everything up one string. The video will help.

The following example, beginning on the fifth fret of the E string, shows how you can take a concept like playing chromatically up and down the fingerboard and make it sound musical.

Ex. 2

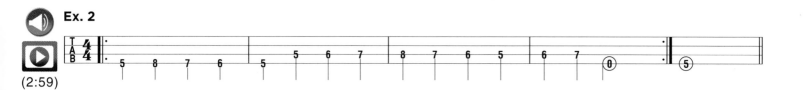

(2:59)

Now play the above example again, starting first on the A string, then on the D string. Refer to the video for help.

Below is another chromatic pattern, this time using the A and D strings. First, focus on getting the notes under your fingers.

Ex. 3

Now we'll vary the rhythm to make it a little more interesting.

Ex. 4

Before continuing, play the previous two examples on the D and G strings. Again, watch the video if you're unsure of anything.

This next example covers a lot of notes in a limited amount of space. It will also give you some practice making octave jumps. Take your time and get it right. This one's fun!

Ex. 5

(4:15)

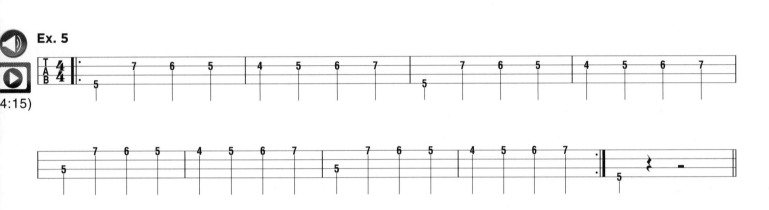

As you practice your chromatics, keep in mind everything we discussed, including making every note ring out clearly, sounding only one note at a time, and making smooth transitions. When you're ready to continue, I've got some more fun stuff I think you're gonna like!

MINOR PENTATONIC SCALE

 Pentatonic scales are among the most popular scales in rock, pop, and many other kinds of music. A pentatonic scale is simply a five-note ("penta" = five) scale. There are all kinds of different pentatonic scales, but in this lesson, we'll focus on the *minor pentatonic scale.* Something about the way this scale is laid out on the fingerboard makes it especially popular with bass players and guitar players, as you'll soon discover.

First, let's get the notes under your fingers. Compared to the previous lessons, you may feel a little bit of a stretch in this exercise as you play the A on the fifth fret and the C on the eighth fret of the E string. But you'll get used to it in no time!

Ex. 1

Now let's play it again. This time, however, we'll vary the rhythm to illustrate just one of the many possibilities with this scale.

Ex. 2

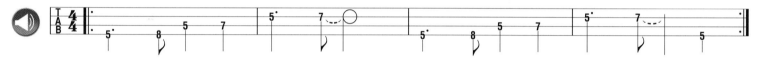

Now try starting at the top of the scale and descending:

Ex. 3

Now with a varied rhythm:

Ex. 4

In this next example, we'll incorporate a position change so as to move up the fingerboard. Notice the fingerings I've indicated here. They'll help you make the transitions more smoothly.

Ex. 5

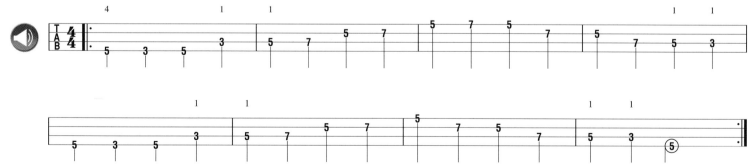

Now, as you may have guessed, we'll play this example again, mixing up the rhythm and making it sound—and **feel**—better!

Ex. 6

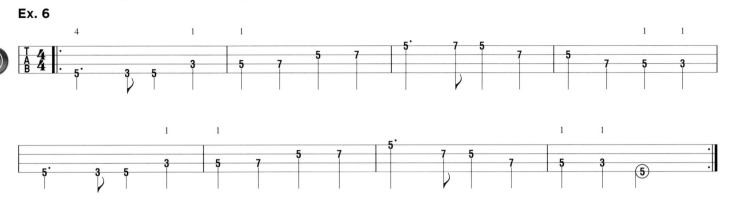

As I mentioned, the minor pentatonic scale is prevalent in pop music. One example, which we'll play next, is Bob Marley's "I Shot the Sheriff," later popularized by Eric Clapton. Practice the following example to get familiar with the notes. Going from the B♭ to the D in measure 3 might feel a little awkward at first, as you'll need to play the B♭ on the E string with your fourth finger and the D on the A string with your third finger. Eventually, your fingers will get used to it. It just takes practice!

Ex. 7

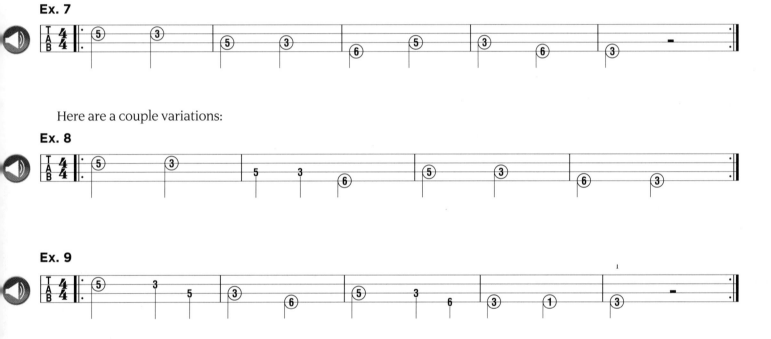

Here are a couple variations:

Ex. 8

Ex. 9

And here is the line itself:

"I Shot the Sheriff"

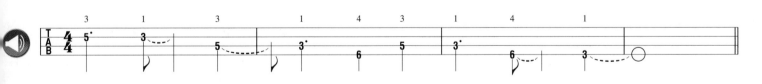

Words and Music by Bob Marley
Copyright © 1974 Fifty-Six Hope Road Music Ltd. and Odnil Music Ltd.
Copyright Renewed
All Rights in North America Administered by Blue Mountain Music Ltd./Irish Town Songs (ASCAP) and throughout the rest of the world by Blue Mountain Music Ltd. (PRS)
All Rights Reserved

Playing pentatonic scales is an absolute must for a bass player. These patterns are a lot of fun and a good basis for improvisation. As you find yourself listening more intently to rock and pop music—especially guitar and bass solos—you'll be able to spot a minor pentatonic scale a mile away!

THE BLUES

Over the years, the blues has become one of the most widely used forms in all of popular music. You hear blues influences in just about every style of music, including rock, jazz, and pop.

In this lesson, we'll begin with the *blues scale*, a very natural transition from the minor pentatonic scale. In fact, the blues scale is the same as the minor pentatonic, except it has one additional note. Not surprisingly, it happens to be the "blusiest" note in the scale!

Here's the blues scale pattern:

Ex. 1

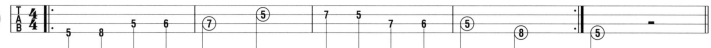

Here's that same scale, but with a varied rhythm:

Ex. 2

Let's practice a few more blues scales and variations.

Ex. 3

Ex. 4

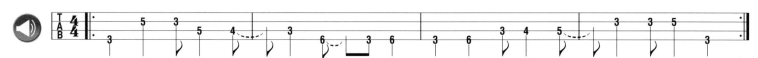

Ex. 5

Ex. 6

The next example illustrates the use of blues scales over an actual 12-bar blues. As you play this one, let your inner blues come out!

Notice the fingerings I've suggested here. Technically, there's no "right" fingering, but I've indicated the way these lines feel most comfortable to me. Sometimes, using your third finger opens up your hand a little, making it easier to facilitate an upcoming stretch, as in bar 2. I've taken this approach several times in this exercise, as well as in the next example. Try these fingerings, but also feel free to experiment to see what works best for you.

Ex. 7

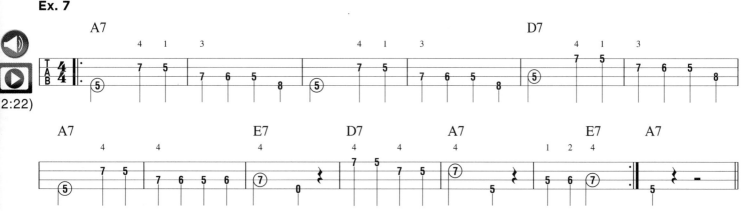

Below is another example of applying blues scales to a 12-bar blues. You may find this one pretty challenging, so start slowly and keep working on it till you get it. As in the previous exercise, I've included some suggested fingerings. Remember to listen to the audio for help.

Ex. 8

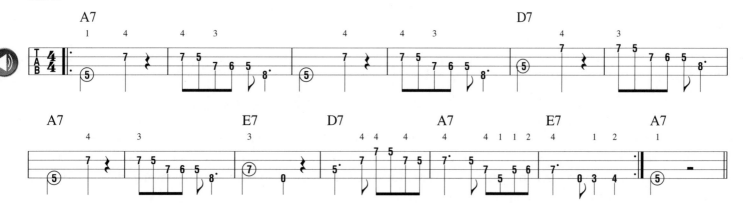

The blues might be the single most requested kind of tune that you'll ever get called upon to play, so make sure you're familiar with the overall form. What's more, there are many different kinds of blues, applicable to just about every genre (jazz, country, rock, pop, etc.). If you're interested in learning more about the blues, I cover a multitude of blues styles—along with history, soloing, and lots more—in my *Blues Bass* book.

LESSON 12

ROCK

There's a rock 'n' roller inside practically every one of us. Chances are, that includes you. In this lesson, we'll go over some beats and grooves that can be applied to several different rock scenarios.

We'll start with a basic rock pattern. First, get yourself familiar with the notes:

Ex. 1

Now, here's the "rocked up" version of the previous exercise. In addition to the varied rhythm, see if you can pick out the minor pentatonic and blues scales.

Ex. 2

(0:52)

In the following example, you'll get some practice playing same-fret 5ths with your pinky, as well as shifting your hand from the fifth and seventh frets down to the third and fifth frets, all in a nice, tidy little rock groove!

Ex. 3

Now, as is our custom, we'll take the same line and play with the rhythms a bit.

Ex. 4

Oftentimes in rock (and other styles), you'll find yourself playing arpeggiated bass lines. The following example, reminiscent of some of what we covered in Lesson 6, is comprised of an A major arpeggio and an A7 arpeggio. As you transition from bar 1 to bar 2, and from bar 5 to bar 6, you'll need to make a same-fret 5–1 maneuver with your pinky. Take your time and work on it until it becomes second nature.

Ex. 5

Now let's play a rock-oriented version of the previous example.

Ex. 6

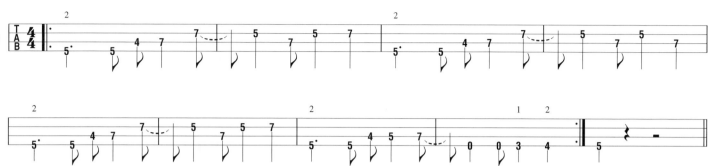

Below is another popular bass line, this one from the White Stripes tune "Seven Nation Army." First, let's make sure you've got the notes under your fingers.

Notice that the following three examples are identical, note-wise. The difference, indicated by the tab, is the positions and the fingerings. The first version has you playing in the low range of the fingerboard, using open strings. The second version has you playing on frets 5 and 7 (see my remarks about fingerings in Lesson 11). The third version has you starting on the seventh fret and playing the entire passage on the A and E strings.

Ex. 7

Now let's play the actual bass line from "Seven Nation Army" with all three variations. Notice I've taken the music notation up just a notch. Nothing to worry about! The first two beats of each bar are made up of a dotted quarter note and an eighth note. This means we hold the first note (the dotted quarter) for one and-a-half beats and the second note (the eighth note) for half a beat. The rhythm in beat 3 is built on exactly the same formula, except that each note is exactly half the duration of the previous notes.

Remember, in Lesson 1, we talked about how beats are divided into whole notes, half notes, quarter notes, and eighth notes? Well, here we're simply taking that formula one step further: half the value of an eighth note is... a sixteenth note. There are four sixteenth notes in each beat. Take a look at the third note, G, in each bar. Since it is a dotted eighth note, we hold it for the length of one and a half eighth notes, the equivalent of three sixteenth notes. The next note, E, completes the value of beat three by providing the fourth sixteenth note. It's really not as complicated as it sounds. As in all the examples, you'll feel it as soon as you hear it. Also, don't let the tie throw you off between beats 3 and 4. Just think of it as one more step toward making you a great sight reader!

"Seven Nation Army"

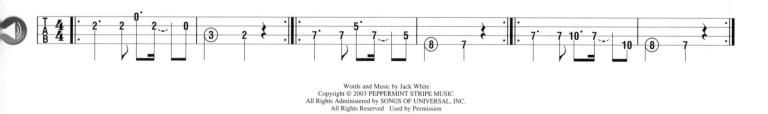

Words and Music by Jack White
Copyright © 2003 PEPPERMINT STRIPE MUSIC
All Rights Administered by SONGS OF UNIVERSAL, INC.
All Rights Reserved   Used by Permission

While this lesson provides some of the basics of rock bass playing, keep in mind that every style of music, including rock, is about injecting the right feel and attitude. Ultimately, it all comes from plenty of listening and practicing, so be sure to do your homework. It's a lot of fun!

FUNK

Another style that's often a sure-fire crowd pleaser is funk. There are several ways to play funk, including slapping, fingerstyle, and others. Here, we'll focus on some simple funk lines, making use of space, syncopation, and injecting just the right notes and feel.

Play this first example until you're comfortable with it. There are some small position changes, so be sure to approach them diligently.

Ex. 1

(0:47)

Now let's "nasty" it up a little with some funk attitude.

Ex. 2

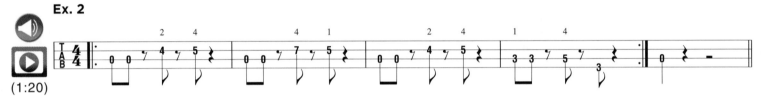

(1:20)

Practice this next example till you've got it down. Watch out for that jump to the low Bb on beat 1 of measure 4.

Ex. 3

And now, funkified...

Ex. 4

As you practice this next line, pay special attention to the fingerings and position shifts, as well as the same-fret 5–1 move in the last bar.

Ex. 5

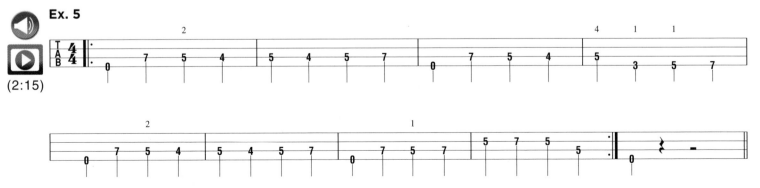

(2:15)

Now let's make it funky. Use the audio to get the feel and to help you with the rhythms and *syncopation*—in which the "ands" of the beats (*upbeats*) are emphasized.

Ex. 6

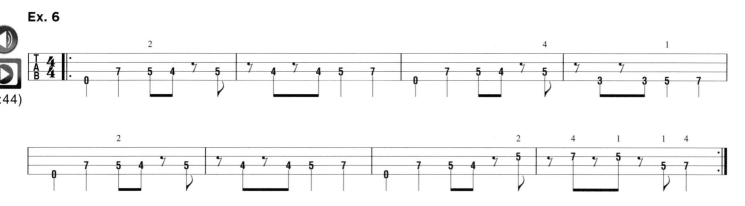

One of the all-time classic funk bass lines is "Super Freak" by Rick James (interestingly, the same bass line was also used nearly a decade later in MC Hammer's "U Can't Touch This"). First, here are a few simplified lines to help you get used to playing the notes:

Ex. 7

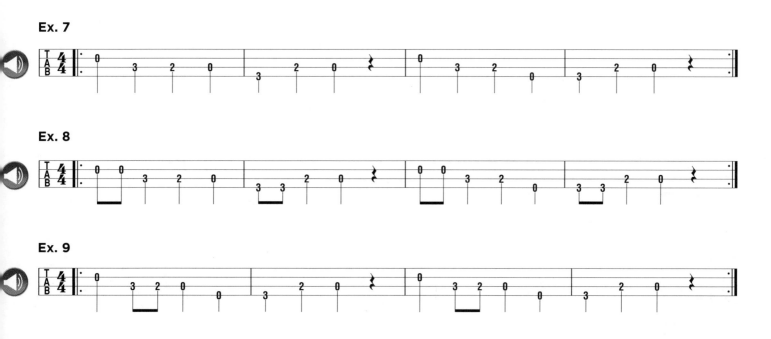

Ex. 8

Ex. 9

And here's the actual bass line. Play it funky!

"Super Freak"

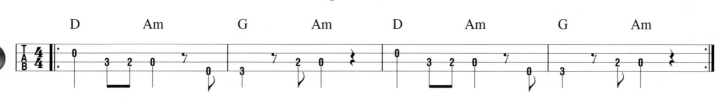

Words and Music by Rick James and Alonzo Miller
Copyright © 1981 Jobete Music Co., Inc. and Stone Diamond Music Corp.
All Rights Administered by Sony/ATV Music Publishing LLC, 424 Church Street, Suite 1200, Nashville, TN 37219
International Copyright Secured   All Rights Reserved

Funk is an important style to have in your arsenal of musical genres. While technique is important, it's even more important to make the music feel good. So, always keep the style in mind. In this case, remember elements like the use of space, syncopation, and your overall funk attitude. When you're ready for a change of pace, move on to Lesson 14 and we'll do something completely different...

SWING/SHUFFLE

Another must-know style in many musical situations is the swing/shuffle feel. While jazz and swing music were all the rage in the early part of the 20th century, their influences have since permeated just about every style of music, including blues, rock, country, and more. Similar to—but **very** different than—funk, there's something about a shuffle groove that makes people react in a certain way. In this case, it's shaking their heads, tapping their feet, and snapping their fingers.

First, let's get acclimated to the *swing/shuffle feel* with the following example. The swing/shuffle feel affects 8th notes by creating a "lopsided" groove. Within a beat, the first 8th note is played longer than the second, as opposed to the evenly divided beat heard in a typical *straight 8th* rhythm (as we've been playing so far). You've probably heard the swing/shuffle feel countless times in music, most commonly in blues and jazz. Check out the accompanying audio and video and you'll recognize it!

Ex. 1

Now let's play this pattern again, first on the D string, then on the G string.

Ex. 2

Ex. 3

The following example is a 12-bar blues, which we'll play with a swing/shuffle feel. Even though it's mostly quarter notes, you still need to bring out the shuffle feel. You'll also get some practice with your chromatic runs and playing across the fingerboard.

Ex. 4

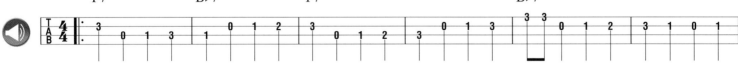

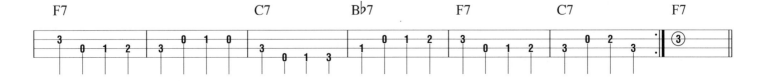

The next example is a variation of the arpeggios we introduced in Lessons 6 and 12. Here, though, you'll notice the F♯ (fourth fret of the D string) gives it a different flavor.

Ex. 5

Now let's play that example again, this time over a D7 chord, beginning on the A string.

Ex. 6

Below is a blues shuffle that will do you well in a country bar, blues club, jazz joint... even a bar mitzvah! Concentrate on making every note ring out clearly. Remember: **every** note is important!

Ex. 7

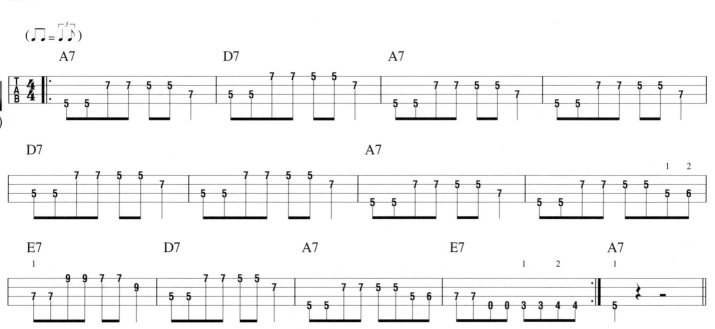

Regardless of how long it's been around, the swing/shuffle style never seems to go out of style. Concentrate on making the music swing and feel good. If you find yourself asking, "How did that feel?" then you're not there yet. Keep at it. Watch for the swayin' and boppin', too. You'll know when you've got it!

LESSON 15

Demo   Play-Along   **"GET READY"**

For this last lesson, I've arranged a version of the Temptations' Motown classic "Get Ready" (later covered by Rare Earth). I took a few liberties with James Jamerson's original bass line to serve the purposes of this book (forgive me, James!). I call your attention to the fills in the last bar of the first chorus; the fourth, eighth, and 12th bars of the second verse; and the bar leading into the saxophone solo. Be sure to pay careful attention to the repeat signs. And remember, if it's too fast, you can slow down the audio to a tempo that's more appropriate.

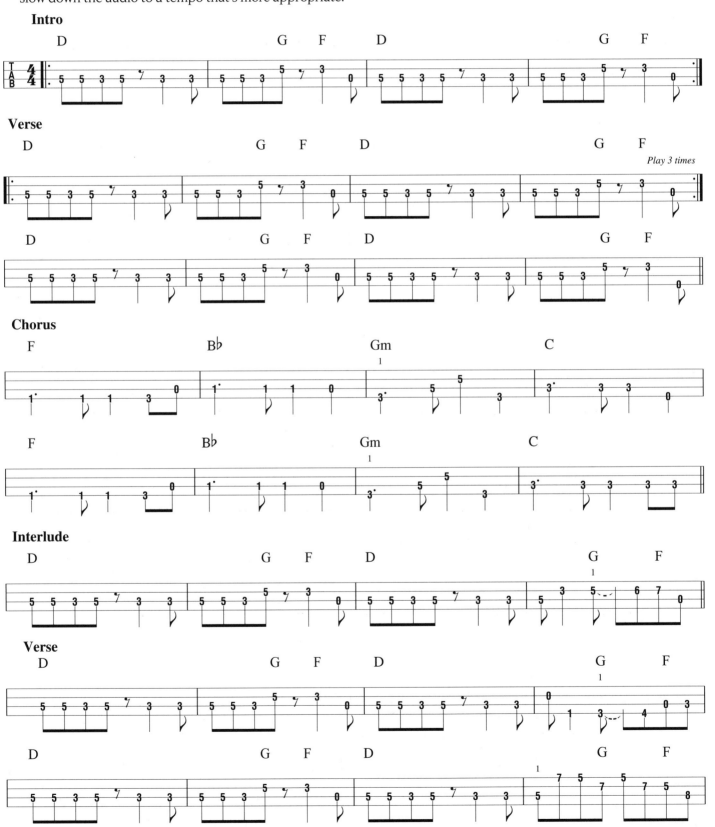

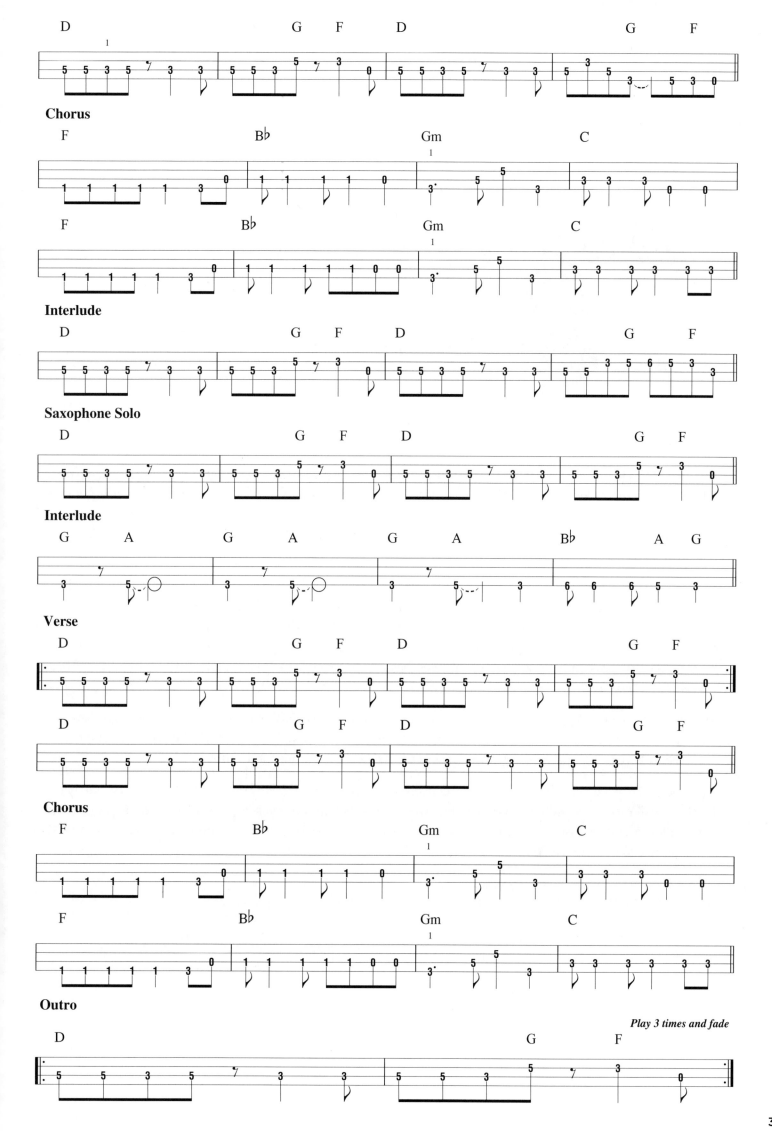

Chorus

Interlude

Saxophone Solo

Interlude

Verse

Chorus

Outro

Play 3 times and fade

ABOUT THE AUTHOR

Jon Liebman is a world-renowned bassist, composer, arranger, author, and educator. He has played electric and acoustic bass in every imaginable setting, from jazz gigs and club dates to full-scale concerts and internationally broadcast radio and TV shows. Jon has performed in many of the world's major concert venues, including New York's Madison Square Garden, L.A.'s Shrine Auditorium, and Tokyo's spectacular Suntory Hall—not to mention bullrings in Central America, amphitheaters in the Caribbean, and all kinds of off-beat settings across the globe.

Throughout the course of a career that began over 30 years ago, Jon has performed and/or toured with a wide range of musical acts, including: Amy Grant, Cleo Laine, Buddy DeFranco, Billy Eckstine, Eartha Kitt, the Drifters, the Platters, the Coasters, the Chiffons, the Ink Spots, the Fifth Dimension, Julio Iglesias, José Feliciano, Ira Sullivan, Ralphe Armstrong, Chita Rivera, Theodore Bikel, and countless others.

He has performed in the pit orchestras of many Broadway shows, including *Dreamgirls, Ain't Misbehavin', Phantom of the Opera, Les Misérables, Fiddler on the Roof, Oliver!, A Funny Thing Happened on the Way to the Forum, Golden Boy, Kiss of the Spider Woman, Annie*, and many others. He's also supplied the bass tracks for major recording projects for clients such as Ford, GM, and the NBA. In addition, Jon has had his big-band arrangements performed on *The Tonight Show, The Late Show*, and other programs.

As an educator, Jon's best-selling books and highly acclaimed online instruction series have helped hundreds of thousands of bass players and are part of the curricula of many music schools, colleges, and universities throughout the world. In addition to the *First 15 Lessons You Should Take on Bass*, Liebman is the author of *Funk Bass, Funk/Fusion Bass, Rock Bass, Blues Bass, Bass Grooves: The Ultimate Collection, Bass Aerobics*, and *Play Like Jaco Pastorius: The Ultimate Bass Lesson*, as well as a book of transcriptions of the music of fellow bassist and friend Stuart Hamm. Jon also performed all the bass tracks on Hal Leonard's *Jaco Pastorius Play-Along* book.

Jon holds a Bachelor of Music degree in Jazz Studies & Contemporary Media from Wayne State University in Detroit and a Master of Music degree in Studio Music & Jazz from the University of Miami in Coral Gables, Florida. Jon has spent time in California, where he was active in the Los Angeles music scene as a performer and writer.

As founder of Notehead MediaGroup, LLC, Jon conceived and developed the very popular *ForBassPlayersOnly.com* and *ForGuitarPlayersOnly.com* websites, as well as his own bass instruction site, *JonLiebman.com*. He has interviewed hundreds of bass players and is considered an authority on the instrument, its history, and its players. Jon lives in Michigan with his wife, Mindy, and has four children.